Piano Solo

THE WORLD'S GREAT CL.

MW01152837

Chopin Piano Music

52 Intermediate to Advanced Pieces

EDITED BY RICHARD WALTERS

Cover Painting: Jean-Baptiste-Camille Corot, *L'atelier de Corot*, ca. 1873

ISBN 978-1-4234-8121-8

HAL•LEONARD®
CORPORATION
7777 W. BLUEMOUND RD. P.O. BOX 13819 MILWAUKEE, WI 53213

Visit Hal Leonard Online at
www.halleonard.com

CONTENTS

Polonaises

Waltzes

Preludes

Prelude in A minor

Fryderyk Chopin
1810–1849
Op. 28, No. 2

Prelude in E minor

Fryderyk Chopin
1810–1849
Op. 28, No. 4

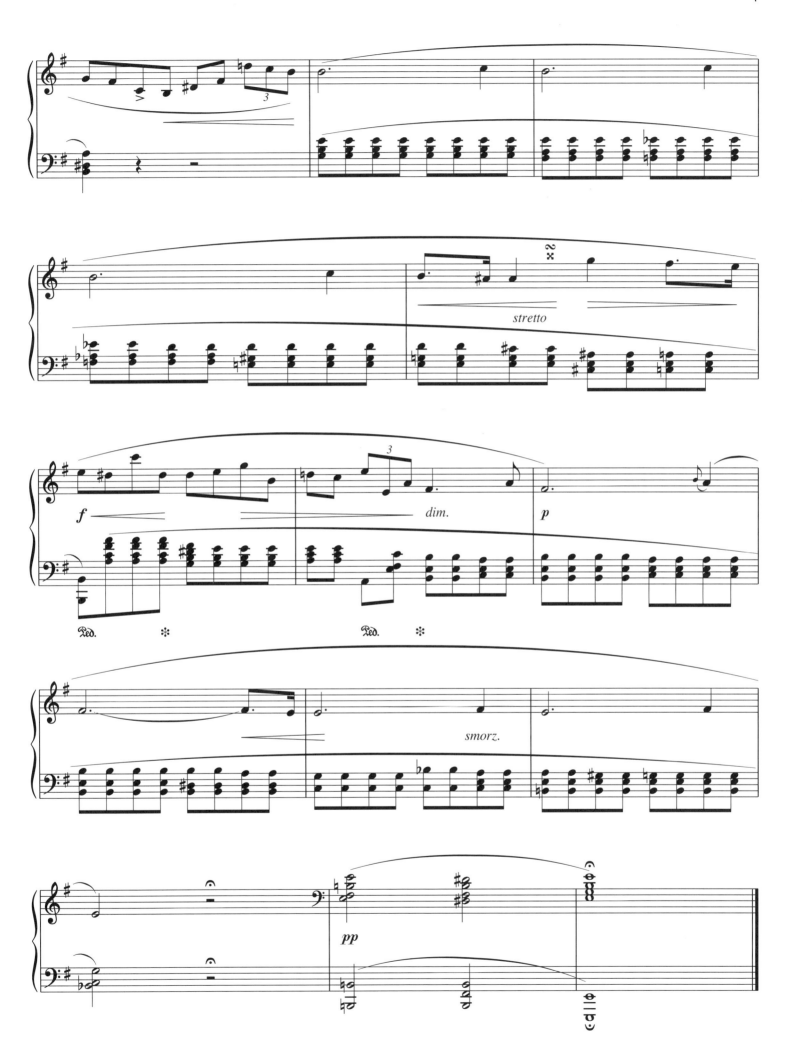

Prelude in B minor

Fryderyk Chopin
1810–1849
Op. 28, No. 6

Prelude in A Major

Fryderyk Chopin
1810–1849
Op. 28, No. 7

Prelude in E Major

Fryderyk Chopin
1810–1849
Op. 28, No. 9

Prelude in F-sharp Major

Fryderyk Chopin
1810–1849
Op. 28, No. 13

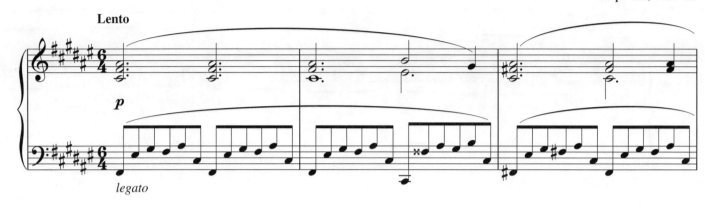

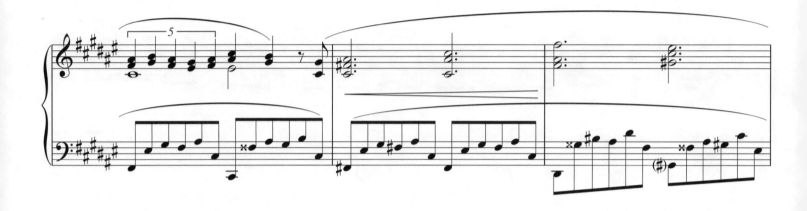

Prelude in A-flat Major

Fryderyk Chopin
1810–1849
Op. 28, No. 17

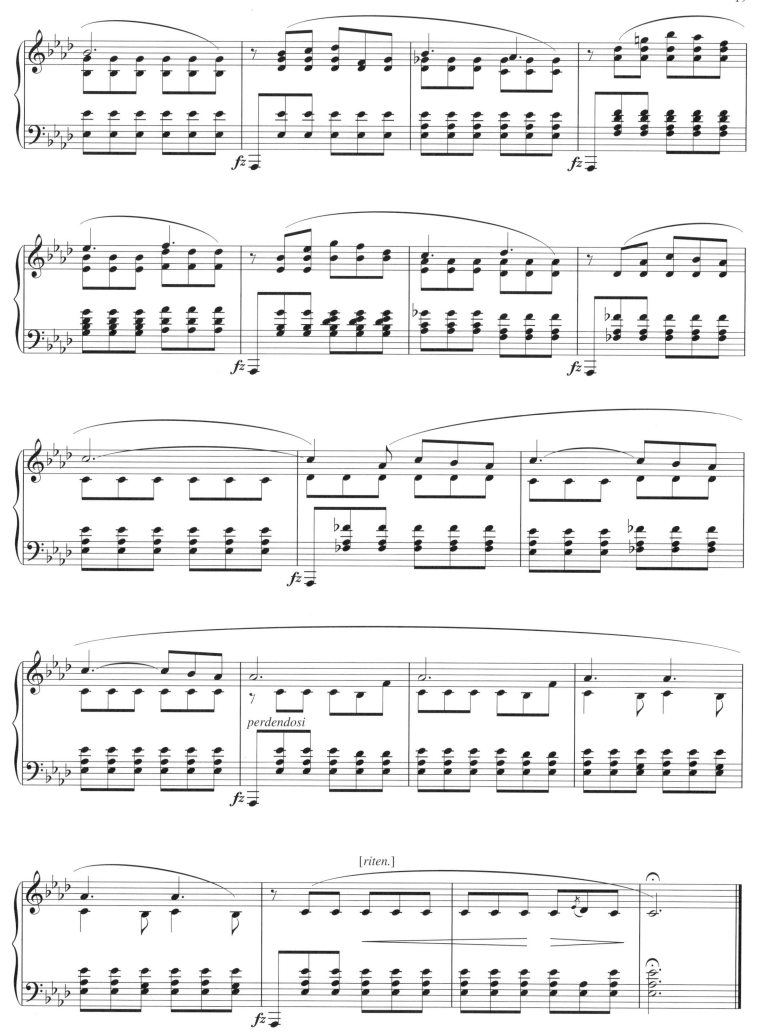

Prelude in D-flat Major

"Raindrop"

Fryderyk Chopin
1810–1849
Op. 28, No. 15

Prelude in C minor

Fryderyk Chopin
1810–1849
Op. 28, No. 20

Prelude in B-flat Major

Fryderyk Chopin
1810–1849
Op. 28, No. 21

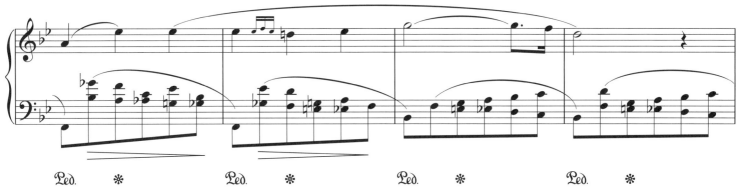

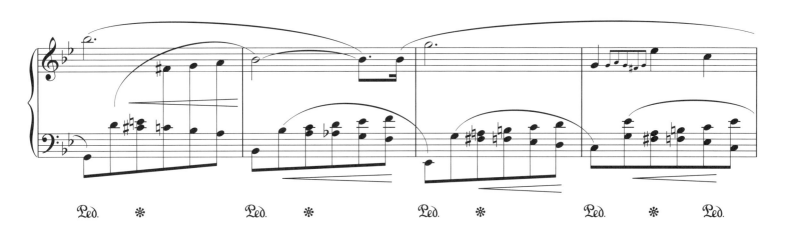

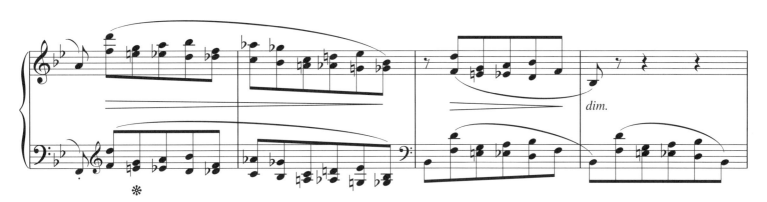

Prelude in G minor

Fryderyk Chopin
1810–1849
Op. 28, No. 22

Prelude in C-sharp minor

Fryderyk Chopin
1810–1849
Op. 45

Mazurkas

Mazurka in F-sharp minor

Fryderyk Chopin
1810–1849
Op. 6, No. 1

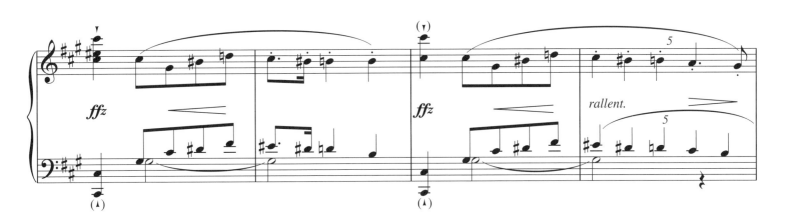

Tempo I

Mazurka in B-flat Major

Fryderyk Chopin
1810–1849
Op. 7, No. 1

Mazurka in C Major

Frederyk Chopin
1810–1849
Op. 7, No. 5

Dal segno senza Fine

Mazurka in A minor

Fryderyk Chopin
1810–1849
Op. 7, No. 2

D.C. al Fine

Mazurka in E minor

Fryderyk Chopin
1810–1849
Op. 17, No. 2

Lento, ma non troppo ♩ = 144

Mazurka in G minor

Fryderyk Chopin
1810–1849
Op. 24, No. 1

Mazurka in A minor

Fryderyk Chopin
1810–1849
Op. 17, No. 4

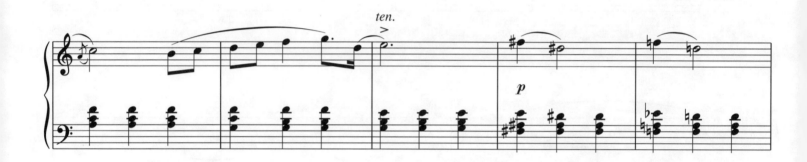

sotto voce

sempre più piano

calando

perdendosi

Mazurka in A-flat Major

Fryderyk Chopin
1810–1849
Op. 24, No. 3

Mazurka in B minor

Fryderyk Chopin
1810–1849
Op. 30, No. 2

Mazurka in F minor

Fryderyk Chopin
1810–1849
Op. 63, No. 2

Mazurka in C Major

Fryderyk Chopin
1810–1849
Op. 33, No. 3

Mazurka in G minor

Fryderyk Chopin
1810–1849
Op. 67, No. 2 (Posthumous)

Mazurka in C Major

Fryderyk Chopin
1810–1849
Op. 67, No. 3 (Posthumous)

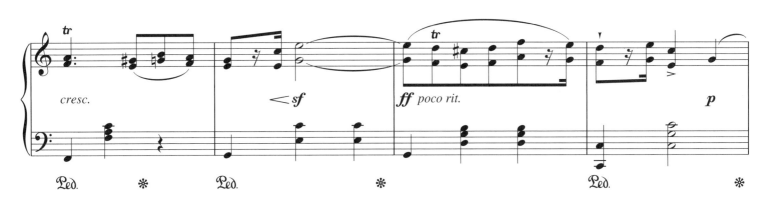

Mazurka in A minor

Fryderyk Chopin
1810–1849
Op. 67, No. 4 (Posthumous)

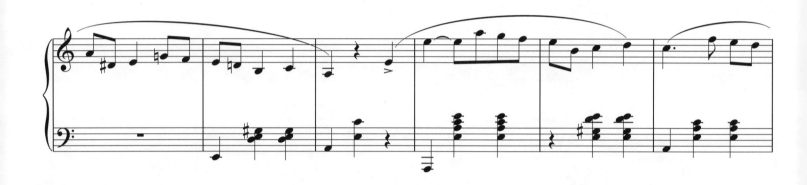

Mazurka in A minor

Fryderyk Chopin
1810–1849
Op. 68, No. 2 (Posthumous)

poco a poco riten.

Tempo I

a tempo

rit.

Mazurka in F Major

Fryderyk Chopin
1810–1849
Op. 68, No. 3 (Posthumous)

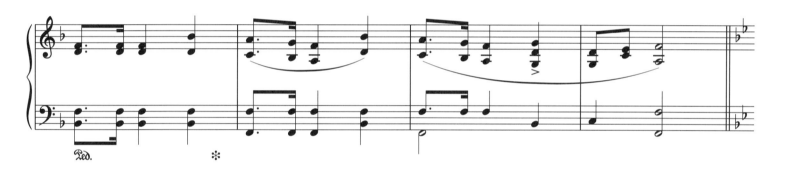

Poco più vivo

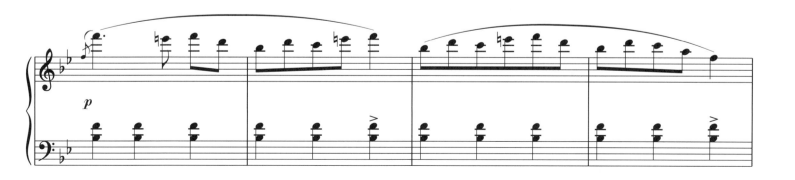

Tempo I

Nocturnes

Nocturne in E-flat Major

Fryderyk Chopin
1810–1849
Op. 9, No. 2

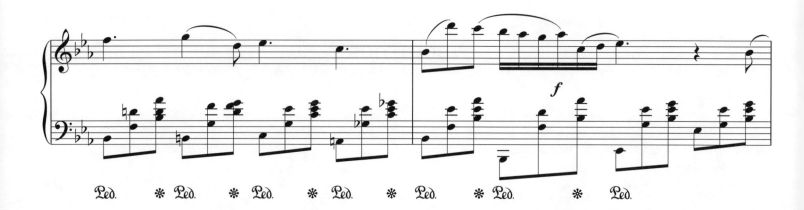

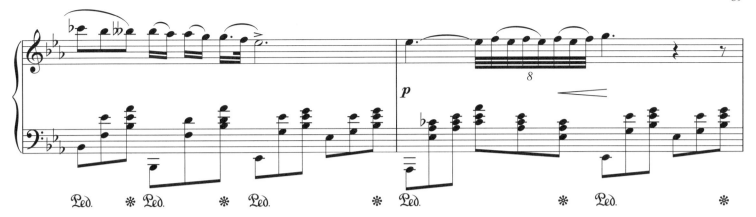

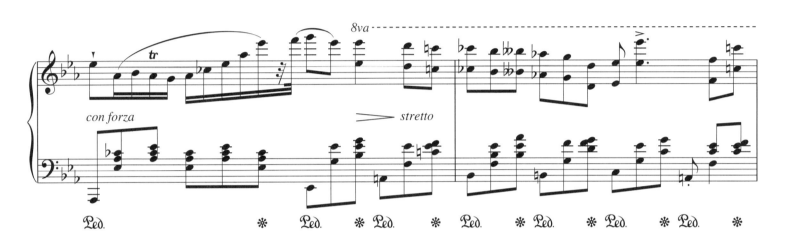

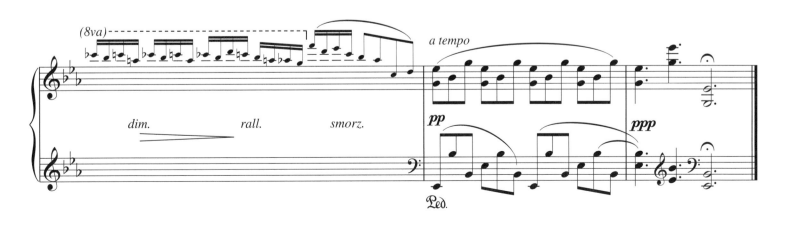

Nocturne in G minor

Fryderyk Chopin
1810–1849
Op. 15, No. 3

Nocturne in B Major

Fryderyk Chopin
1810–1849
Op. 32, No. 1

Nocturne in G minor

Fryderyk Chopin
1810–1849
Op. 37, No. 1

Andante sostenuto

Nocturne in F minor

Fryderyk Chopin
1810–1849
Op. 55, No. 1

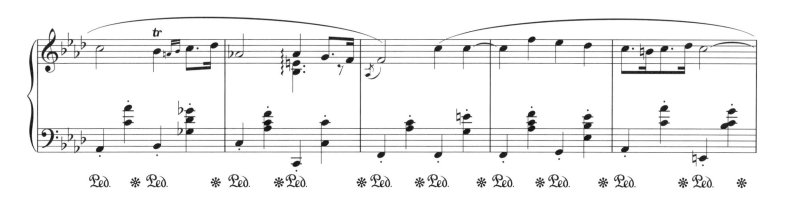

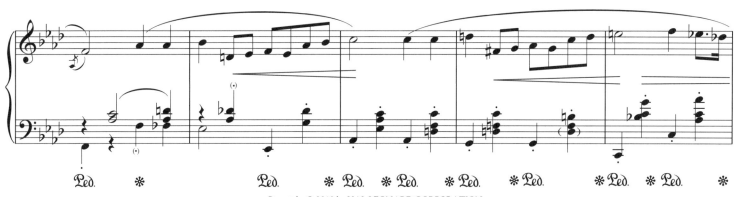

Nocturne in C minor

Fryderyk Chopin
1810–1849
Op. 48, No. 1

Nocturne in E minor

Frédéric Chopin
1810–1849
Op. 72, No. 1 (Posthumous)

Nocturne in C minor

Fryderyk Chopin
1810–1849
KK IVb, No. 8 (Posthumous)

Nocturne in C-sharp minor

Fryderyk Chopin
1810–1849
KK Anh. Ia, No. 6 (Posthumous)

(This page has been intentionally left blank.)

Polonaises

Polonaise in C-sharp minor

Fryderyk Chopin
1810–1849
Op. 26, No. 1

Fine

(D.C. senza repetizione sin' al Fine)

Polonaise in A Major
"Militaire"

Fryderyk Chopin
1810–1849
Op. 40, No. 1

Allegro con brio

Polonaise in C minor

Fryderyk Chopin
1810–1849
Op. 40, No. 2

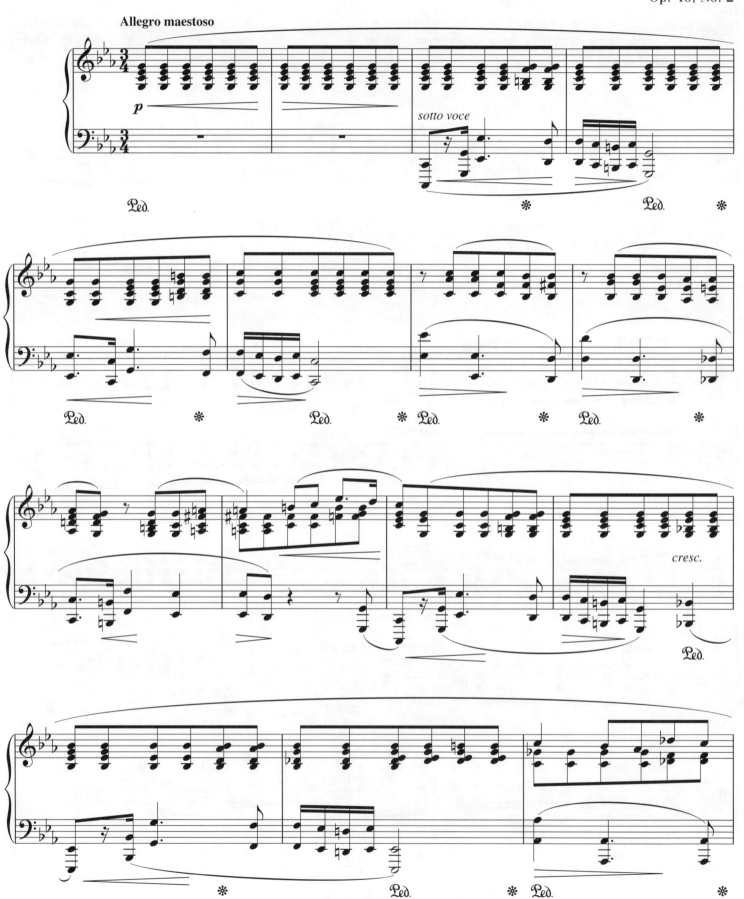

Polonaise in G minor

Fryderyk Chopin
1810–1849
KK IIa, No. 1 (Posthumous)

(Fine)

Trio

(Polonaise da capo sin' al Fine)

Polonaise in B-flat Major

Fryderyk Chopin
1810–1849
KK IVa, No. 1 (Posthumous)

(Fine)

Trio

(Polonaise da capo sin' al Fine)

Waltzes

Grand Waltz Brillante in E-flat Major

Fryderyk Chopin
1810–1849
Op.18

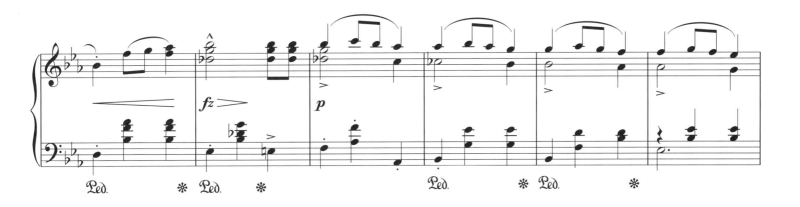

Ped. ✻ Ped. ✻ Ped. ✻ Ped. ✻ Ped. ✻

Ped. ✻ Ped. ✻ Ped. ✻ Ped. ✻ Ped. ✻

(Ped. ✻)

con anima

Ped.   Ped.   Ped.

Ped.   (Ped.

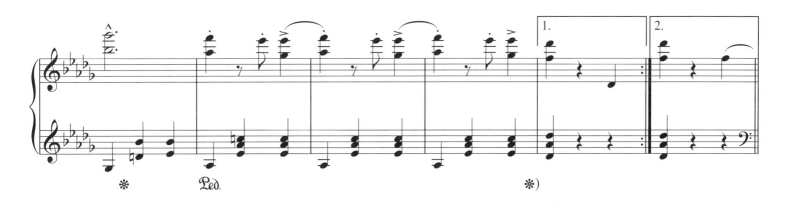

Ped.

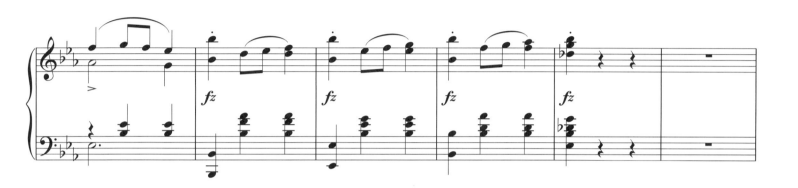

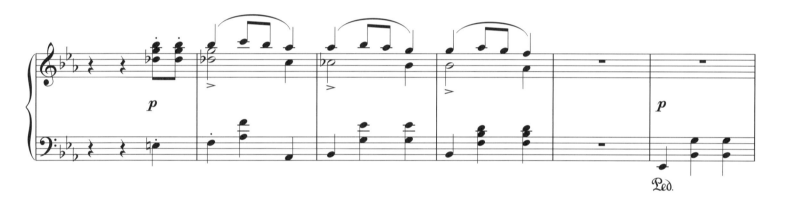

Grand Waltz Brillante in A minor

Fryderyk Chopin
1810–1849
Op. 34, No. 2

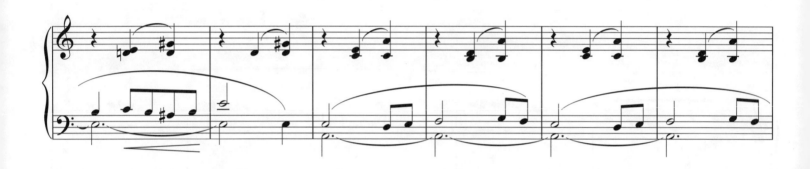

Waltz in D-flat Major
"Minute Waltz"

Fryderyk Chopin
1810–1849
Op. 64, No. 1

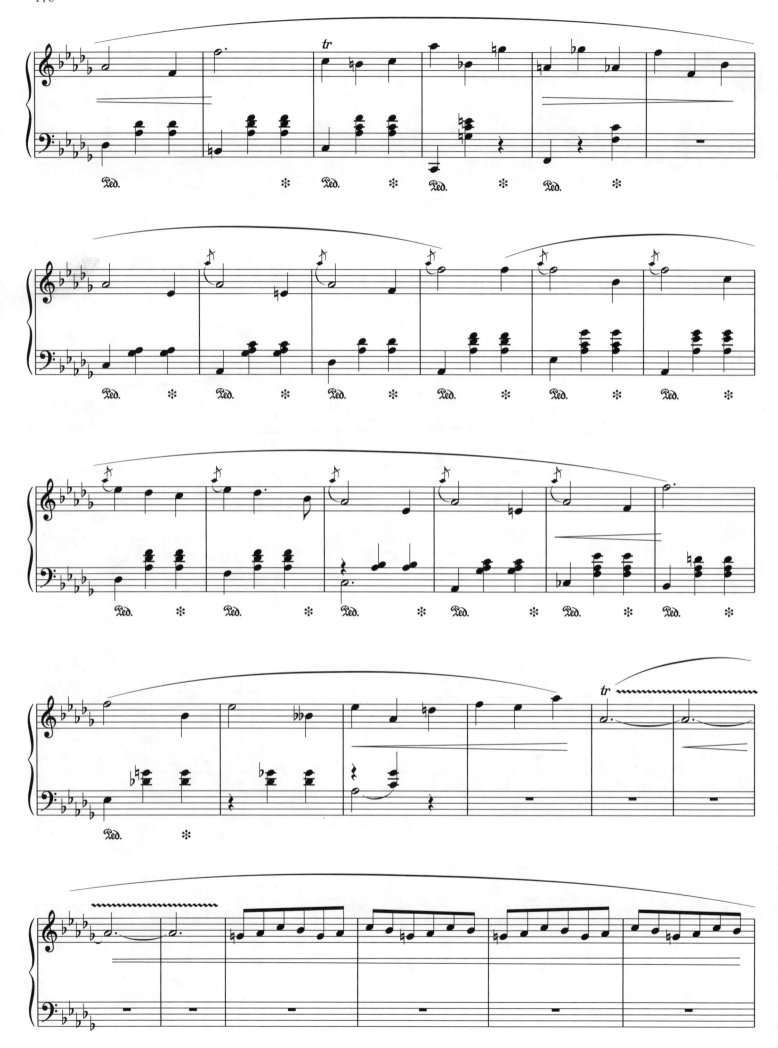

Waltz in A-flat Major

Fryderyk Chopin
1810–1849
Op. 64, No. 3

Waltz in C-sharp minor

Fryderyk Chopin
1810–1849
Op. 64, No. 2

Tempo giusto

Più mosso

Waltz in A-flat Major

Fryderyk Chopin
1810–1849
Op. 69, No. 1 (Posthumous)

Waltz in B minor

Fryderyk Chopin
1810–1849
Op. 69, No. 2 (Posthumous)

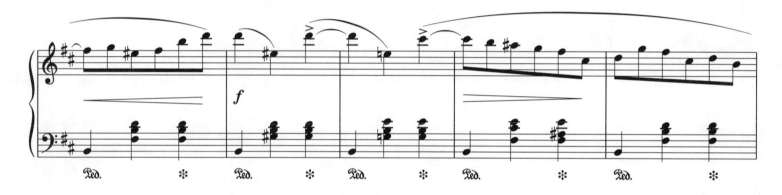

Waltz in F minor

Fryderyk Chopin
1810–1849
Op. 70, No. 2 (Posthumous)

Waltz in E minor

Fryderyk Chopin
1810–1849
KK IVa, No. 15 (Posthumous)

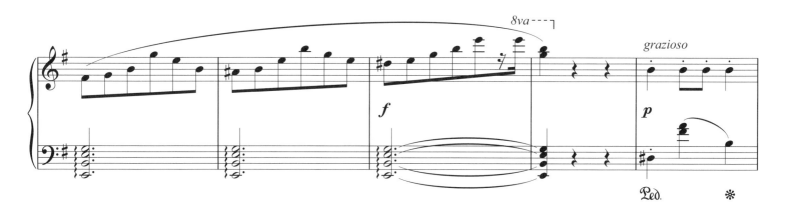

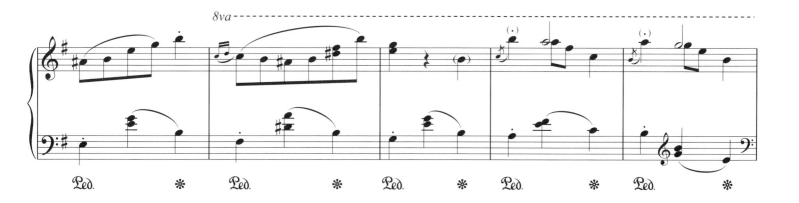

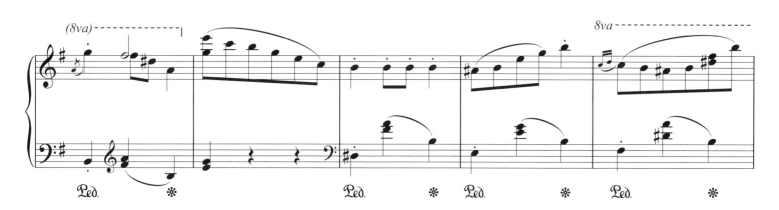

(This page has been intentionally left blank.)

Fantaisie-Impromptu in C-sharp minor

Fryderyk Chopin
1810-1849
Op. 66

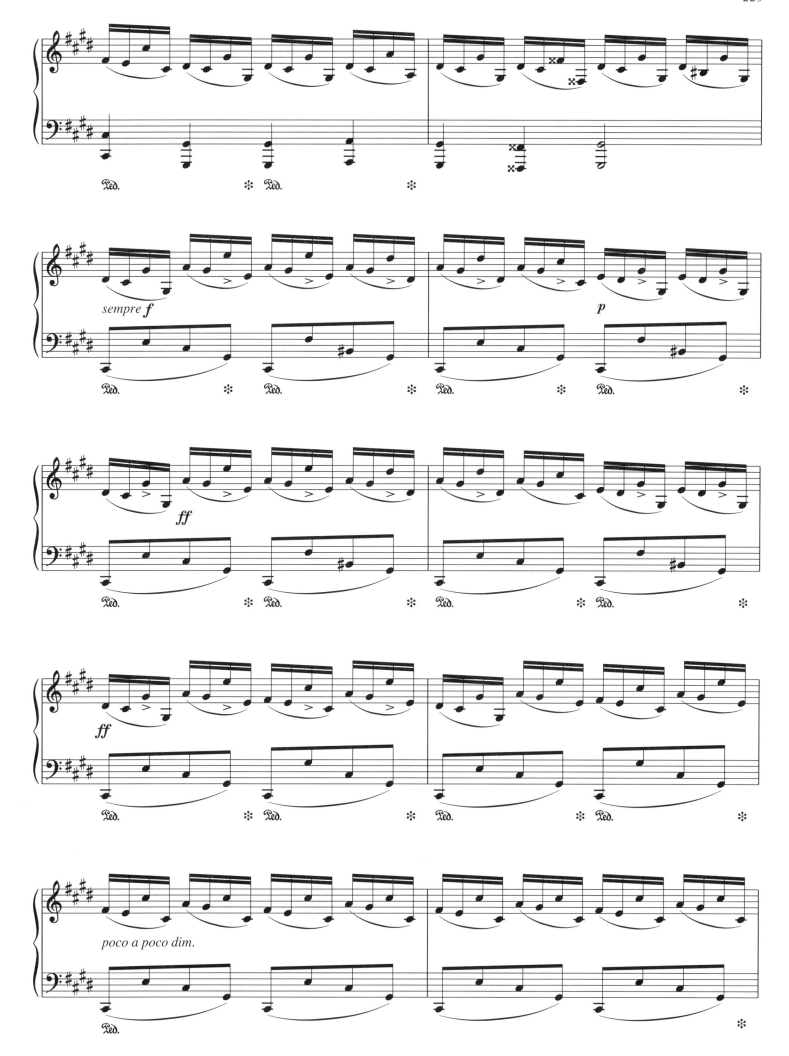

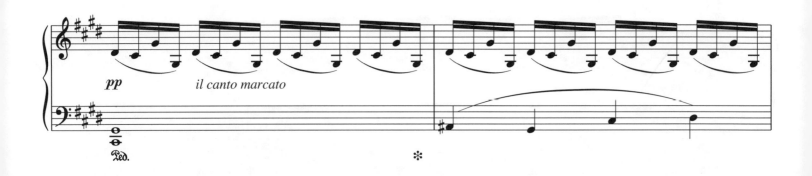

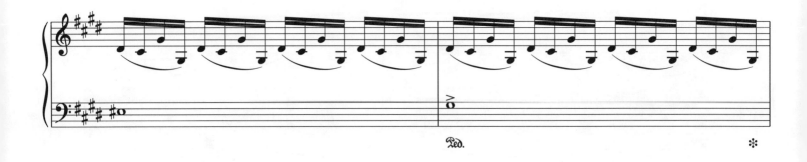

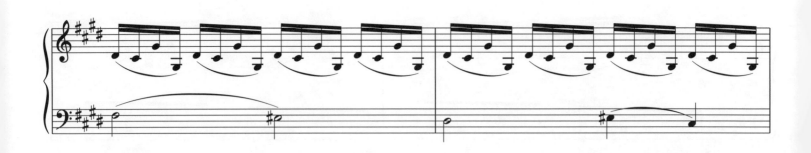

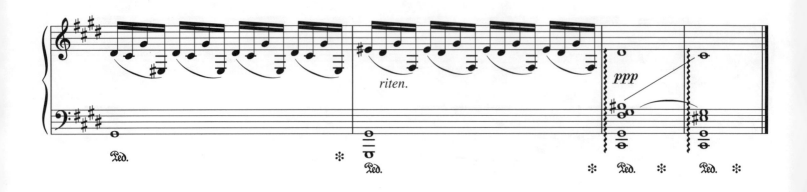